John Dillinger

Public Enemy:
America's Most
Notorious Gangsters

Roger Harrington

Copyright © 2017.

All rights reserved. No part of this publication may be reproduced, distributed, or transmitted in any form or by any means, including photocopying, recording, or other electronic or mechanical methods, without the prior written permission of the publisher, except in the case of brief quotations embodied in critical reviews and certain other noncommercial uses permitted by copyright law.

This book is intended for informational and entertainment purposes only. The publisher limits all liability arising from this work to the fullest extent of the law.

Table of Contents

Introduction

Early Life

Jail Time

First Robberies

Lima Jail Break and Dillinger Gang Robberies

Crown Point Jail Break and the second Dillinger Gang

Lincoln Court Shootout

Little Bohemia Lodge

Public Enemy #1

Plastic Surgery

The Last Days of The Dillinger Gang

Betrayal and Death

Conclusion

Introduction

In the period following World War 1, America enjoyed a period of extreme prosperity. The "Roaring Twenties" saw a boost in industry and production, as well as a new, more relaxed lifestyle. Americans indulged in hot jazz music, illegal speakeasies, and reckless spending.

The prosperity led to stock market speculation. Speculation means that people were buying stocks for products they assumed would increase in value due to the widespread prosperity and overproduction. It also meant that people were buying and selling arbitrary stocks while they were very valuable, regardless of history of the company, or what the stock represented. It was an economic bubble. Banks were also doling out easy credit to many individuals looking for more money to back the artificially inflated stocks.

The economic boom meant that farms and industries were able to wildly over-produce their products. However, as is explained by the rule of supply and demand, too many of the same product on the market means that each individual product is devalued.

America could not go on giving credit to people who bought over-inflated stocks for companies that were over-producing their products. The bubble had to burst. London's stock market crashed on September 20th, 1929, leading to a panic in America. Stocks were shaky, and the economy was on the verge of tanking. Despite numerous attempts to inject capital into stocks to save the economy, as was done during the 1907 crisis, the market still fluctuated uneasily. Individuals and companies alike began to sell their stock at a rapid rate.

On "Black Monday", October 28th, 1929, the DOW fell by 38.33 points, or 13%, as a selling panic began. On October 29th, 1929, now famously known as "Black Tuesday", a record number of stocks were traded, and the DOW fell by an additional 30 points, or 12%.

Thus began the Great Depression. Investment in American industry dropped dramatically, leading to a decline in the once-booming industry. This, in turn, lead to unemployment as plants and factories had to be shut down; leading further to a marked lack of spending by the American people. It is estimated that as many as 15 million Americans were out of work at this time.

Banks were closing with great speed and taking customers' money with them. Nearly half of America's banks were forced to close during the crisis. Many citizens were without jobs or steady incomes. It was one of the worst economic climates in American history. The us/them mentality was stronger than ever as common people turned against the remaining banks, considering them to be heartless institutions that stole money from loyal customers while the American people suffered en masse.

Outlaws like Bonnie and Clyde, and "Pretty Boy" Floyd became heroes in the eyes of the American people. These people rolled up to banks and demanded money; a feat that many destitute Americans dreamed they could do. The robbers were considered Robin Hood type characters; giving the evil, rich banks what they deserved after treating their customers so poorly. However, these thieves weren't stealing from the rich to give to the poor, as Robin Hood did; they were stealing from the rich to line their own pockets.

Nevertheless, as newspapers continued to report on the exploits of the outlaws they became celebrities in their own right; as recognizable and idolized as any movie star. It was the perfect environment for the handsome, charming, and cunning John Dillinger to round up a gang of robbers and take the American banks by storm.

Early Life

John Herbert Dillinger was born on June 22, 1903 in Indianapolis, Indiana. His mother, Mary Ellen Lancaster, died of a stroke when John was only three years old. His father, John Wilson Dillinger, owned a small grocery store in the city. John Sr. was a religious man, who reportedly alternated between abusing and spoiling his son; beating him, then giving him money for treats, or locking him in the house, then allowing him to stay out all night.

After his mother died, John was largely raised by his older sister, Audrey and her husband until their father remarried in 1912. There are rumors, though unsubstantiated, that John hated his stepmother at first, but the two eventually grew closer and began a three-year sexual relationship.

John's teenage years were filled with fights, various petty crimes, and all night parties. He even had a childhood gang he dubbed The Dirty Dozen who terrorized younger children, vandalized, and stole. He earned the nickname Jackrabbit for how spry he was, and how nimbly he evaded the police.

John quit school at the age of 16 and began working in a machine shop. Though he was a good worker, he continued his hard-partying lifestyle. John still liked staying out all night and committing crime.

John Sr. grew tired of his son's misdemeanors, and worried about his future. He decided to sell his grocery store and move the family to a small town, in the hopes that getting away from the corrupting influence of the big city would help his son settle down and stay out of trouble. In 1921 the Dillingers moved to Mooresville, Indiana.

John Sr. did not get his wish. His son continued to commit petty crimes and live his wild lifestyle. Soon after the family moved, John was arrested for auto theft. He then made his first of what would be many escapes from police custody. Knowing the police were after him and that he could not return home, John Dillinger enlisted in the U.S Navy.

Dillinger made it through basic training and was posted on the now-famous U.S.S Utah, the ship that was sunk during the 1941 Pearl Harbor attacks. Dillinger was not exactly a regimented rule follower. He resented the strict, by-the-book lifestyle he was supposed to lead and, when the ship was docked in Boston, Dillinger deserted, only 5 months after he enlisted. John was eventually dishonorably discharged from the U.S Navy.

Dillinger made his way back to Mooresville in 1924, where he met and married 16-year-old Beryl Hovious. The couple, being young and unemployed, moved in with Dillinger's father. John just couldn't stay away from the criminal lifestyle. He was once arrested for stealing chickens. John Sr. was able to smooth things over with the owner and the matter was settled out of court. The already strained father-son relationship got worse.

John and Beryl then moved to her parents' home in Martinsville, Indiana. John got a job in an upholstery shop, and began playing shortstop on the neighborhood baseball team. On the field he met Ed Singleton, another petty criminal, and a distant relative of his stepmother's. Singleton was Dillinger's first partner in crime. The two men began a robbery plot.

Singleton knew of a grocer who would be carrying his weekly receipts on him after work. He said John could easily rob the man, while Singleton worked as the getaway driver. John carried a .32 caliber pistol, and a large metal bolt wrapped in a handkerchief.

The plan was to hit the grocer over the head with the bolt, knock him out, and take his money. Instead, when John struck the grocer, the man put up a fight and, in the ensuing chaos, the pistol accidentally discharged.

John then assumed he had shot the man, and ran to find Singleton. Some accounts say that the two men attempted the robbery together, were recognized by a local pastor, and turned in to the police. Some say John attempted to robbery alone, and when he went to take his getaway car, Singleton was nowhere to be found, leaving John to wander the streets and eventually be picked up on suspicion by the local cops.

Regardless, Dillinger and Singleton were eventually caught by police and brought before a judge. Although Singleton had a previous criminal record, he was also equipped with competent legal counsel. The man pleaded not guilty and received a sentence of two years in jail. Singleton would later die after passing out drunk on a railroad track.

The prosecutor told John Sr. that if his son were to plead guilty, he would receive a lenient sentence. Dillinger went in front of the judge without a lawyer. Assuming he would just receive a slap on the wrist he took his father's advice to plead guilty. However, he didn't receive the leniency he was told to expect. In a surprising turn of events, John Dillinger was convicted of assault and battery with intent to rob, and received a sentence of 10 to 20 years of jail time, to be served in the Indiana State Reformatory.

This was a truly shocking sentence for a comparatively paltry crime. Embittered with the prospect of facing so many years in prison, John was quoted as saying, "I will be the meanest bastard you ever saw when I get out of here."

Jail Time

Dillinger was incarcerated in Indiana State Reformatory in 1924. He played on the prison baseball team, and was a model worker at the prison's shirt factory. Accounts say he routinely finished his own quota quickly, and worked to fulfill the quotas of his fellow workers. This, and his charming personality, made him popular among other inmates.

He was, however, far from a model prisoner. Dillinger tried to escape several times, and befriended many hardened criminals who began to educate him on the ins and outs of robbing banks. For Dillinger, the old idea that prison is just criminal school was beyond true. The legend of John Dillinger began in prison. He would never have reached such a celebrity status without the knowledge he gained and the men he met in Indiana State Reformatory.

At first Dillinger's wife, Beryl Hovious, wrote and visited him frequently. After a while, though, she became weary of the distance between her and her husband. She was still very young, and facing the possibility of up to twenty years without her husband weighed heavily on her. She began visiting and writing less frequently, and eventually filed for divorce on June 20th, 1929, just two days before John's 26th birthday. Dillinger was devastated. Soon after this crushing event, he was denied parole. John was to stay in prison to at least serve the minimum time he was given. Dillinger became even more despondent.

He asked to be transferred to Indiana State Prison, from the Indiana State Reformatory. The Prison was stricter on inmates and much more regimented. Prison officials were unsure why a man who had so much trouble with authority would ask to be moved to a harsher environment. When asked, John claimed the prison had a better baseball team. Still suspicious of his motives, but not willing to pass up an opportunity to give Dillinger a stricter environment, officials approved the transfer.

Dillinger didn't end up joining the prison baseball team. Instead, he teamed up with his friends from the reformatory, Harry

Pierpont, and Homer Van Meter, who had been transferred a few months prior. Career criminals with no intention of letting prison reform them, the men were already planning a jailbreak, and several bank robberies for when they got out of jail.

Dillinger and his crew also met Walter Dietrich, a man who had worked with one of the most notorious bank robbers of the time, Herman Lamm. Dietrich taught the men the meticulous methods used by Lamm to pull off successful heists. Lamm was known for doing detailed research before hitting a bank. He knew the bank layout, the location of all the valuables, the movements of the guards and workers, and where the nearest police station was.

Pierpont and Van Meter had the knowledge and the plans in place, but they still needed to actually get out of jail to go ahead with their perfectly-crafted robberies. To do that they would need a man on the outside to outfit them with guns, and money to bankroll the escape. John had a significantly smaller sentence than his friends and would be getting out much earlier. Pierpont and Van Meter brought Dillinger on to aid them in their escape. They informed Dillinger of reliable accomplices and safe houses, and gave him a list of banks and stores that would be good bets to rob.

The plan was fast-tracked in May of 1933 when Dillinger's stepmother fell ill. He was released on parole on May 10th, 1933 after serving only nine and a half years of his ten to twenty year sentence. His stepmother died before he arrived home, but at least John was free.

First Robberies

John Dillinger was released from prison at the height of The Great Depression. With no legitimate job prospects to fall back on, and his friends in prison relying on him for escape, he immediately turned to crime again. Just six weeks after his release he committed his first bank robbery to begin to get the money necessary to break his friends out of jail.

On June 21st, 1933, Dillinger and two unidentified men (most likely members of Pierpont's gang) robbed the New Carlisle Bank in New Carlisle, Ohio. The men made off with $10,800. The Dayton Daily News reported that the bandits snuck into the bank at some point during the night, and ambushed the first person to arrive to work that morning, clerk Horace Grisso. Dillinger and his crew bound any bank staff that entered the building while they were waiting for access to the vault.

Dillinger and his accomplices continued in this way; using Herman Lamm's meticulous bank robbing techniques to pull off well-crafted heists.

On July 17th, 1933, Dillinger robbed The Commercial Bank in Daleville, Indiana, making off with $3,500. A few weeks later, on August 4th, he stole $6,400 from the Montpelier National Bank, also in Indiana. Just ten days after that heist he robbed the Bluffton Bank in Ohio of $6,000. Police began tracking Dillinger from that point forward.

He had a distinctive bank robbing style, often displaying his athletic prowess by vaulting smoothly over teller counters.

On September 6th, 1933, Dillinger robbed one last bank to ensure he could carry out the plan. At the Massachusetts Avenue State Bank in Indianapolis, Indiana Dillinger made off with $21,000. He now had sufficient funds to bankroll the prison break. Though his friend Homer Van Meter, who had originally planned the escape, had actually been paroled on May 19th, 1933, the plan was still to go forward, ensuring Pierpont and his gang was made free men.

On September 22nd Dillinger was arrested in connection with the Bluffton robbery after the police received a tip about his whereabouts from the landlady of an old girlfriend John had recently visited. He was sent to a prison in Lima, Ohio to await trial on the charges. While being searched at the prison, guards found a mysterious paper among Dillinger's belongings. It looked like plans for a jailbreak, but Dillinger refused to explain the paper's significance.

Four days later, on September 26th, 1933, ten men Dillinger met in Indiana State Prison used the jailbreak plan to escape. Dillinger had used the money from the bank heists to buy weapons and bribe key figures at the prison. He smuggled seven .45 caliber pistols into the prison in a barrel of thread meant for the on-site shirt factory.

Harry Pierpont and Russell Clark told the shirt factory superintendent, George Stevens, he was needed in the basement. There he was jumped by the rest of the gang and taken hostage. Walter Dietrich went and found deputy superintendent Albert E. Evans and claimed he needed the man's help to break up a fight in the factory basement. Evans was also jumped by the gang and became their second hostage.

Pierpont had been harshly disciplined by Evans during his stay at the prison. He used this opportunity to get revenge on the man who had terrorized him for months. Dietrich actually had to stop Pierpont from going too far and severely hurting, or killing Evans; more because it would put a kink in their plan than because he had any respect for Evans' life.

Foreman Dudley Triplett happened to be heading to the basement for supplies and, though he was not part of the original plan, was also taken hostage. Luckily for the criminals, their gang was large enough to deal with the need to take surprise hostages.

The men made Stevens lead the way through the prison. They concealed their guns under stacks of shirts and slowly made their way through the prison. The rest of the guards and prisoners didn't seem to notice what was going on.

There were four gates standing between the men and their freedom. At the first gate

Stevens was forced to tell the guard, Frank Swanson, to let the party through, or they would kill him. Swanson became yet another hostage. The gang got through the second gate in the same way, with more threats of violent death. At the third gate they used a metal shaft from the factory as a battering ram, and burst open the door themselves.

Guard Fred Wellnitz was badly beaten until another guard, Guy Burklow, opened the outer gate of the prison. The men and their hostages were now in the lobby of the prison's administration building. The gang herded the eight prison workers they found there into the prison's vaults. Joe Burns shot 72-year-old Finley Carson twice for not moving fast enough.

At that moment, the warden, Louis E. Kunkel, came into the lobby. He was made to join the rest of the workers in the vaults. The gang then walked out the front door of the prison.

Harry Pierpont, Charles Makley, Russell Clark, Ed Shouse, John Hamilton, Walter Dietrich, James Clark, Joseph Fox, Joe Burns, and Jim Jenkins were now free men.

Dietrich, James Clark, Fox, and Burns went one way. They immediately ran into Sheriff Charles Neel who had just performed a prisoner intake in the administration building. The men overpowered him, stole his weapons, and took him hostage. They forced him to drive them away from the prison. They abandoned the sheriff's car near

Wheeler, Indiana, and stole another vehicle, which quickly blew a tire. The men were now on foot, and lost in a dense, wet forest.

Eventually the group began to see their hostage, Sheriff Neel, as a burden. They fought over what to do with him. James Clark was also becoming troublesome to the rest of the group, complaining of stomach problems. Neel and Clark split from the group. Clark released Neel in Gary, Indiana, and the lawman immediately had Clark arrested and sent right back to prison.

Pierpont, Russell Clark, Ed Shouse, John Hamilton, Charles Makley, and Jim Jenkins all went another direction when they escaped the prison. They had help from the outside and went to gang accomplice Mary

Kinder's house. She had agreed to help the men find safe houses and evade the law if they would include her brother, Earl Northern, in the escape plan. Northern, however, was in the infirmary at the time of the escape and had to be abandoned.

Kinder still followed through on her promise to help the men, and set them up with new clothes, and a hideout in Hamilton, Ohio. Most of the men in Pierpont's group would soon join Dillinger and come to be known as The Dillinger Gang. Unfortunately for Jenkins, while on the way to their safe house in Hamilton, the men had to evade the police. During a chase the car door swung open and Jenkins fell out. The rest of the men couldn't risk going back for him. He was killed that night.

Pierpont, Shouse, Clark, Hamilton and Makley got safely to Ohio where they used the hideout in Hamilton, as well as Pierpont's parent's house, to plan yet another jail break.

Lima Jail Break and Dillinger Gang Robberies

Now that Dillinger's friends were out of prison, they planned to return the favor, and spring John from the Lima jail.

On October 12th, 1933, Harry Pierpont, Charles Makley, and Russell Clark, all recent escapees from Indiana State Prison thanks to Dillinger, embarked on a mission to free their friend from where he was being held in Lima, Ohio.

Sheriff Jess Sarber and his family lived in a house on the same grounds as the jail. He, along with his wife and Deputy Wilbur Sharp, had just finished dinner, and had moved to the Sheriff's office to talk. Pierpont, Makley and Clark came to the office claiming to be police officers needing to transfer Dillinger back to Indiana State Prison in connection with outstanding charges at his previous place of incarceration.

Sheriff Sarber, asked the men for credentials that would corroborate their story. Pierpont then fired his gun twice, hitting the sheriff once. The men took the keys to Dillinger's cell, and locked the deputy and the sheriff's wife in the basement to ensure a quick and uninterrupted escape. Sheriff Sarber died of his wounds about two hours after he was shot.

Dillinger, Pierpont, Makley, and Clark fled to Chicago to meet up with the rest of the gang. They plunged headfirst into a life of crime. Realizing they would need much more firepower to pull off the robberies they had planned, the gang decided to raid a police arsenal for supplies.

They used the same detail-oriented approach they used in bank robbing when they cased the arsenal. It turned out the stash was poorly guarded and would be easily taken over by Dillinger and his crew. They raided the arsenal and made off with multiple guns, a load of ammo, and bullet proof vests.

The men then embarked on a spree of bank robberies. They hit the Home Banking Company in Saint Mary's, Ohio for $12,000.

A few weeks later they stole $74,802 from the Central National Bank & Trust Company in Greencastle, Indiana. Just a month later they hit the American Bank & Trust Company in Racine, Wisconsin, making off with $28,000.

By this point the gang was infamous. The way they went about their business in an almost gentlemanly manner gained them great popularity among the American people.

The gang always wore suits and fedoras to their robberies, and was generally gracious to the bank's customers and workers. No drug or alcohol use was permitted during the planning or carrying out of any robbery, leaving no room for error. The men split the loot evenly and planned heists meticulously.

They were consummate professionals, often keeping business hours when planning and executing their robberies, then going home to their families just like legitimate businessmen.

John Dillinger's name was even used to sell cars in ads that claimed Dillinger would never be caught if he continued to drive a Ford.

Chicago police were becoming increasingly agitated by both the existence of The Dillinger Gang, and their growing popularity. On December 14th, 1933, Detective William Shanley was following up on a tip that the Dillinger Squad may have been responsible for a robbery committed the previous day. Shanley approached John

Hamilton at a garage where he was having his car detailed. Hamilton shot and killed Shanley, then escaped.

Chicago police set up a taskforce made up of as many as 40 men, led by Melvin Purvis. They were called The Dillinger Squad, and their one task was to find The Dillinger Gang and bring them to justice for their robberies and the murder of Detective Shanley.

Things started going south for the gang on January 15th of 1934. While Makley, Pierpont, and Clark were lying low in Tucson, Arizona, Dillinger and Hamilton planned a heist of the First National Bank in East Chicago, Indiana. During the robbery, Dillinger got into an altercation with Officer William Patrick O'Malley and ended up shooting him eight times in the chest, killing him. The men still managed to steal $20,000, but Dillinger was now wanted for murder.

Dillinger and Hamilton journeyed to Tucson to meet back up with the rest of the gang. They were staying at the Hotel Congress when a fire broke out on January 21st, 1934. All guests were forced to evacuate the hotel. Some members of the gang had to be rescued through a window, and down a fire truck ladder.

They were not permitted to bring their luggage but, as the gang had guns and money in their bags, they did not want to leave the luggage to burn up in a fire. Makley and Clark tipped firemen $12 each to go back and get their valuable luggage. Among them was William Benedict

A few days later, Benedict was reading a copy of True Detective, a true crime magazine, and recognized the men who asked him to retrieve their luggage. He told police the gang had been in town. Tracing the luggage firemen had pulled from the building, police found Makley's bags at a gang safe house, 927 North Second Avenue. On January 25th police went to the residence and took Clark into custody.

Makley was followed by police and arrested at the Grabbe Electric and Radio store where he was attempting to buy a radio that would pick up police frequencies. Pierpont was caught in a staged traffic stop, lured to the police station, and arrested. Dillinger was also taken into custody at the same safe house police found Clark. All together the police found $25,000 in cash and several stolen guns on the captured gang members.

A debate ensued between all the states where the men were wanted criminals. Since the gang had hit banks in Ohio, Indiana, and Wisconsin, all three states wanted to extradite the men and bring them to justice in their state.

Pierpont, Makley, and Clark were sent to Ohio to stand trial for Sheriff Sarber's murder.

Ed Shouse, one of the escapees from Indiana State Prison, and ex-member of the Dillinger gang, testified against Pierpont, Makley, and Clark. His testimony helped rack up charges against the gang members. In the end, both Pierpont and Mackley were sentenced to death, and Clark was given life in prison.

On September 22nd, 1934 Pierpont and Makley attempted yet another jailbreak. Makley was shot dead in the escape attempt. Pierpont was wounded, but survived, and was executed as planned on October 17th. Clark spent much of the rest of his life in prison. He was released on medical parole in 1968, but only survived a few months out of prison. He died of cancer on Christmas Eve, 1968.

Crown Point Jail Break and the second Dillinger Gang

Dillinger was extradited to Crown Point, Indiana where he was supposed to stand trial for Officer O'Malley's death. He was placed in the Crown Point jail that local police deemed "escape-proof". The sheriff held a press conference outside the jail where she and several important members of local law enforcement were photographed palling around with Dillinger.

There are differing accounts of what happened next, but one thing is certain, Dillinger proved the jail was definitely not escape-proof.

One account says Dillinger's crooked lawyer managed to smuggle a gun into John's cell, which he then used to break out. Another account says he fashioned a wooden gun out of a shelf in his cell. Yet another account claims Dillinger carved a gun out of either a bar of soap, or a potato, and blackened it with boot polish.

Whether the gun was real or not, the guards on duty on March 3rd, 1934, believed it was. Dillinger and another prisoner, Herbert Youngblood, escaped from Crown Point jail with a guard as a hostage. Security around the prison had been relaxed from where it was when Dillinger first arrived, and the men were able to walk the streets unseen and unbothered.

Dillinger and Youngblood took the guard to a local garage where they took a worker as another hostage, and stole a car that belonged to the county sheriff.

It was then that John Dillinger made a mistake that would ultimately lead to his downfall. He drove the stolen car across the Indiana-Illinois state border, violating the National Motor Vehicle Theft Act. The Bureau of Investigation, a precursor to the FBI, could now be involved in the manhunt for Dillinger. It seems odd, with so many robberies, jailbreaks, and even a murder under Dillinger's belt, that this would be the crime that would involve national law enforcement, but it was technically his first federal offense.

J. Edgar Hoover, the director of the Bureau of Investigation, jumped at the chance to hunt down Dillinger. Hoover hated Dillinger's popularity, and the fact that crime was being celebrated in America. Hoover went on to use many of the facts from the Dillinger Gang and other Depression-era outlaws to get the creation of the Federal Bureau of Investigation approved.

Although local and national law enforcement agencies were on the hunt for Dillinger, his biggest problem after escaping from the Crown Point jail was that his faithful gang members, Pierpont, Makley, and Clark were all in prison. Dillinger needed a new gang.

Some reports say that Lester "Baby Face Nelson" Gillis actually helped Dillinger escape from Crown Point in exchange for Dillinger's membership in Nelson's gang. Others say that Dillinger went to his old Indiana State Prison friend Homer Van Meter looking for men to outfit a new gang. Regardless of how it began, two of the most notorious bank robbers of the 1930s were now working together.

The Second Dillinger Gang (as some news outfits dubbed it due to Dillinger's popularity) consisted of Dillinger, Nelson, Van Meter, John Hamilton, Tommy Carroll, and Eddie Green. This gang was a far cry from the calculated and meticulous First Dillinger Gang. Nelson was known as a hothead who enjoyed getting into fights, and enjoyed firing his gun.

The first robberies committed by the new gang did not go as smoothly as earlier robberies. On March 6th, 1934 the men hit Securities National Bank & Trust in Sioux Falls, South Dakota. All the gang members were doing their jobs: Carroll was on lookout outside the bank, Hamilton sat in the car ready for a getaway, Dillinger, Van Meter, Green and Nelson all entered the bank to perform their assigned duties.

Of Nelson, Tommy Carroll was quoted as saying, "That guy would walk into hell and back on a job. He's a mental case otherwise, but he would fight the devil when we were hitting a bank". He proved that to be true during this heist.

Nelson saw a motorcycle patrolman, Hale Keith, through the window. He stood on a cashier's counter and fired his gun, laughing while he shot. Nelson hit the man several times. Luckily Keith survived, but this violent and entirely unprovoked attack was unprecedented for a Dillinger Gang robbery. Other shootings had at least been ostensibly in self-defense, or to serve a purpose. They didn't shoot innocent people. But Nelson just enjoyed chaos.

Taking the $49,500 they scored from the bank, the gang surrounded themselves with hostages and bystanders on the way to their car. The waiting police didn't dare attempt to take out any gang members when they were so close to innocent civilians. The gang made five of their hostages stand on the car's running boards to create a human shield as they drove away.

One Officer managed to shoot the car's radiator before the gang drove out of sight. This slowed the car down a few miles outside of town. Three police cars caught up to them, but retreated in the ensuing hail of gunfire. The gang hijacked another vehicle, drove the hostages ten miles out of town, released them, and escaped.

Despite the chaotic robbery and close call with the police, the Second Dillinger Gang immediately began planning another robbery. On March 13th, 1934, just a week after the Sioux Falls heist, the gang hit First National Bank in Mason City, Iowa. Again, Nelson caused trouble. He, Carroll and

Dillinger were stationed outside the bank, while the other men went in to collect the money.

Nelson was firing wildly in different directions for no obvious reason. He ended up hitting bystander R.L James in the leg. Later, when Hamilton came out of the bank he was enraged seeing another innocent person wounded. Nelson, obviously lying, claimed he thought the man was a police officer.

Though his shots were the most arbitrary and destructive, Nelson was far from the only one to fire a gun that day. An off-duty police officer, James Buchanan, saw what was happening at the bank. He grabbed a sawed-off shotgun and took cover nearby.

He didn't want to fire into the crowd that that gathered to watch the robbery, so he just traded insults with Dillinger, who was guarding the bank door.

Something Buchanan said must have rubbed Dillinger the wrong way. That or he just got bored of the interaction. Dillinger pulled his .38 pistol from his pocket and fired, missing Buchanan. Carroll also fired his weapon at an oncoming car that quickly backed up and fled the scene.

All the gunfire caught the attention of Judge John C. Shipley who was working in his third floor office above the bank. He appeared at the window to see what the commotion was, and Dillinger fired up a volley of shots to warn Shipley to keep out of it. Shipley went to his desk, retrieved his pistol, and shot Dillinger in the shoulder.

After the men left the bank with $52,000, Shipley once again fired at the gang members. This time he managed to hit Hamilton, also in the shoulder. Like the Sioux Falls robbery, the gang managed to get away thanks to a human shield of hostages. Dillinger and Hamilton visited Dr, Nels Mortensen in the middle of the night to have their wounds attended to.

Lincoln Court Shootout

On March 20th 1934, Dillinger moved into the Lincoln Court Apartments in St. Paul, Minnesota, with his girlfriend, Evelyn "Billie" Frechette. The couple used the aliases Mr. and Mrs. Carl T. Hellman.

The Lincoln Court landlady, Daisy Coffey, was immediately suspicious of the couple. They often had parties that would last all night, and were frequently visited by other suspicious individuals. Coffey said she spent much of the Hellmans' stay in apartment 310, which allowed her to look into their apartment, number 303, from across the courtyard.

Eventually Coffey decided to let the Minnesota branch of the Bureau of Investigation know of the odd happenings in apartment 303. Lincoln Court was then put under surveillance by Agent Rufus Coulter, and Agent Rusty Nalls.

On March 31st, 1934 the two agents, along with St. Paul police detective Henry Cummings, continued to surveil the complex, looking for the Hudson sedan Coffey had made note of to the Bureau.

Coulter and Cummings then went up to apartment 303 to talk to the suspicious tenants. Billie Frechette answered the door, cracking it only a few inches. She told the men she wasn't dressed and they would have to wait a few minutes. Nalls, seated in the car downstairs, saw Homer Van Meter pull up and enter the apartment complex.

Coulter went to use a phone and inform the Bureau of their attempt to engage with whoever was in the apartment. He returned to wait for Billie to open the apartment door, when Van Meter suddenly appeared in the hallway. He evaded the officers' questions and tried to calmly walk back down the stairs. Coulter and Cummings were suspicious of the man, and Coulter followed him to the lobby, where Van Meter opened fire on the agent.

Coulter fled outside where Nalls told him to disable Van Meter's car. Coulter shot out the tires of Van Meter's Ford, but Van Meter still managed to get away, either by hopping on a passing truck, or by carjacking a passerby.

Meanwhile, Billie had realized that the men at the door were law enforcement, and told Dillinger they had been found. After hearing Van Meter's shots from the lobby, Dillinger fired through the door of his apartment into the hallway where Cummings still stood. The officer dove for cover and, when Dillinger came out into the hallway to continue to shoot, Cummings shot back.

There was a significant imbalance of firepower between the men. Dillinger had a Thompson submachine gun, capable of firing off bursts of bullets at a time; while Cummings just had his police revolver that only held five rounds. Cummings shot at

Dillinger, hitting him in the calf with one of his few bullets, and managed to flee down the stairs and out of the building.

Dillinger and Frechette exited the building through a back door, and drove off in their Hudson. They went to Eddie Green's safe house where Dr. Clayton May was called to look at Dillinger's wound. Dillinger was moved to the apartment of Augusta Salt, where May worked on patients he could not see out in the open at his office. He stayed there for five days.

On April 2nd, 1934 Eddie Green visited Dillinger at Salt's apartment. Later that day he would be tracked down and shot by the Bureau of Investigation. He would die of his wounds on April 11th, but not before he made several delirious statements to the Bureau of Investigation.

It was clear that the Bureau of Investigation had a far-reaching influence, and was going to be relentless in their pursuit of Dillinger and his gang. John and Billie decided to go back to Mooresville and stay with John Sr. and reconnect with other Dillinger family members.

Early in the morning of April 7th, John and his half-brother Hubert were in a car accident. The Dillingers were returning from Ohio where they were attempting to visit Harry Pierpont's parents. Hubert fell asleep at the wheel, rammed into another car, and ended up 200 feet in the woods. Both Dillingers fled the scene.

In the car, police found some odd items, including some maps, a length of rope, and a bullwhip. Hubert later said his brother was going to use the bullwhip on his former lawyer, Joseph Ryan, who had disappeared with his retainer.

The party needed a new car. Later that day Billie, Hubert, and Hubert's wife bought a new Ford V8. The next day the Dillingers had a family picnic. The Bureau of Investigation surveilled the picnic. Dillinger knew he was being watched. He escaped by hiding on the floor of Billie's new V8, and having her drive him and several family members from the picnic.

On April 9th, Dillinger and Frechette drove to Chicago to meet up with friends of the

Dillinger Gang, hoping they would help the couple find a safe house. Larry Strong promised to help hide the couple. Larry sent them to his tavern to await details. Billie entered first to make sure it was safe for John. It wasn't. Strong had turned against Dillinger, and police officers were inside the tavern waiting for him. They took Billie into custody.

Dillinger was frantic and panicked knowing he couldn't go into the tavern to help Billie as he would either be arrested along with her, or killed on the spot. He immediately hired his lawyer, Louis Piquett, to take on Billie's case, and often met with him to discuss it.

Billie was given a $1,000 fine, and was sentenced to two years in prison for harboring a fugitive. Dillinger paid her fine for her, though Piquett claimed the money came from Billie's sister, as the very fugitive Billie was in trouble for harboring paying the fine she incurred for harboring him would not look good for her.

John desperately wanted to break Billie out of prison, even going as far as casing to the prison to get a feel of the layout, and robbing a police arsenal in Warsaw, Indiana with Van Meter to acquire the firepower necessary to stage a breakout. Billie and Dillinger's other friends managed to convince him he shouldn't attempt a rescue. He would surely be recognized, and probably killed, if he approached the prison, or made any trouble.

Dillinger and his gang, along with the wives and girlfriends of the members decided to go into hiding somewhere nice and remote where they could all unwind and Dillinger could get his mind off Billie's arrest.

Little Bohemia Lodge

On April 20th, 1934, the whole of the Second Dillinger Gang (Dillinger, Van Meter, Nelson, Carroll, Hamilton, their wives and girlfriends, and gang errand runner Pat Reilly) checked into Little Bohemia Lodge in Manitowish Waters, Wisconsin.

The gang was planning on having a quiet weekend of dining and card playing. They were not to get their wish. The lodge owner, Emil Wanatka, felt something was amiss during a game of cards he was playing with Dillinger, Nelson, and Hamilton. When Dillinger won a hand and stood up to collect his winnings, Wanatka noticed the man wore a shoulder holster. Looking around at his other guests, he saw the rest were similarly armed.

While out in town the next day, Wanatka's wife told a friend, Henry Voss, that they believed The Dillinger Gang was staying at their lodge. Voss called the Bureau to inform them of the whereabouts of the gang, and the layout of Little Bohemia.

Melvin Purvis, not wanting to waste any time, or let the gang get away, immediately mobilized a team to fly from Chicago to Wisconsin. The team planned to simply sneak up to the lodge, and take the gang by surprise. There weren't many roads into the lodge, and the building backed out onto a lake, so Purvis assumed there wouldn't be many ways for gang members to escape the raid.

This was the very early days of the Bureau. There were not yet protocols to follow for this type of raid. No roadblocks had been set up, the local authorities were not informed, and the agents were not completely sure of the layout of the lodge, or who exactly was meant to be there.

That night Little Bohemia Lodge was having a dinner special that attracted around 75 people. Some guests were still leaving just as the agents were driving up. A car leaving the lodge approached the agents, who shouted at the driver to stop and identify himself. The men in the car, John Hoffman, Eugene Boisneau and John Morris, didn't hear the command due to the volume of the radio, and their boisterous conversation.

The agents opened fire on the car, killing Boisneau, and wounding Morris and Hoffman. At that moment, Pat Reilly and a gang member girlfriend Pat Cherrington, were returning from an errand Reilly was running for Van Meter. They saw the trouble with the civilian car and made a hasty break for freedom. The agents shot at Reilly and Cherrington, but the two managed to get away.

All the commotion outside alerted the gang members to the presence of authorities. Dillinger, Van Meter, Hamilton, and Carroll all fled on foot through the back of the lodge and into the woods.

Baby Face Nelson, not being one to shy away from a fight, got into a shootout with the agents. He fled into the woods in the opposite direction of the rest of the gang.

Nelson emerged from the woods just a mile away from the lodge. He kidnapped a couple and forced them to drive him away. Shortly after this he ordered them to pull over again, and entered the home of Alvin Koerner, who had already reported the suspicious car idling outside of his house.

Emil Wanatka and his brother-in-law, George LaPorte, were driving to Koerner's house to borrow coats and supplies for the workers of Little Bohemia, who were being forced to stand around outside in the parking lot due to the raid.

Nelson attempted to take more hostages and steal yet another car. He forced Wanatka and Koerner into LaPorte's car and demanded to be driven away. The car stalled, and Wanatka could not get it to start.

As the men tried to get the car to work again, and Nelson became increasingly agitated, a Bureau vehicle drove up. Agents W. Carter Baum and Jay Newman, and local police officer Carl Christensen were in the car. They were responding to Koerner's tip about the suspicious vehicle parked outside his house.

Nelson asked the men to identify themselves. When they told him they were agents he demanded they get out of the car. Newman and Christensen began to get out of the car, and Nelson opened fire on them.

He shot Newman in the forehead, hit Christensen several times, sending him into a ditch, and fatally wounded Baum with three shots to the neck.

Koerner and Wanatka got out of LaPorte's car and ran for cover. Nelson began firing wildly in different directions attempting to shoot his hostages. He then shot Christensen and Newman again. He hopped into the awaiting Bureau vehicle, and pushed Baum's body out onto the ground before driving away.

Purvis was sure Dillinger and his gang was still hiding somewhere in Little Bohemia. As the sun rose, shining light on Wanatka's bullet-ridden lodge, he told Purvis the gang was sure to have all escaped during the night.

Agents took Nelson's wife Helen, as well as Marie Comforti, and Jean Delaney into custody. They were all found guilty of harboring known criminals, but were released on parole.

Dillinger, Van Meter, and Hamilton all rendezvoused after their escape and managed to commandeer a vehicle. Minnesota police received a tip that the gang might be heading in their direction. They were given a license plate number and car model to watch for. The car was spotted at around 10am, April 23rd, 1934 in St. Paul Minnesota.

St. Paul authorities Joe Heinen, Norman Dieters, Larry Dunn, and Fred McArdle followed the vehicle south to St. Paul Park. There the authorities fired warning shots at Dillinger, Van Meter, and Hamilton. Dillinger fired back, and a chase ensued. Fifty shots were fired altogether, including one by McArdle that severely wounded Hamilton.

Famous underworld doctor, Joseph Moran, refused to treat Hamilton, though he did allow him to use the Barker-Karpis safe house to recuperate. Hamilton died of his wounds on April 27th, and was buried in a gravel pit in Oswego, Illinois by Dillinger, Van Meter, and friends.

Public Enemy #1

The raid on Little Bohemia Lodge was catastrophic for the Bureau of Investigation and for Hoover and Purvis personally. With one Bureau agent, and one civilian dead, many others wounded, and no gang members in custody, the whole operation was a huge disaster. Calls went out for Hoover's resignation and Purvis' suspension. Hoover had to up the efforts to find Dillinger and his murderous companions.

The term Public Enemy first appeared in American law enforcement in April 1930, when Chicago Crime Commission chairman Frank J. Loesch attempted to organize the many gangsters who were popping up during Al Capone's reign in Chicago.

He said of the invention of the list, "I had the operating director of the Chicago Crime Commission bring before me a list of the outstanding hoodlums, known murderers, murderers which you and I know but can't prove, and there were about one hundred of them, and out of this list I selected twenty-eight men. I put Al Capone at the head and his brother next, and ran down the twenty-eight, every man being really an outlaw. I called them Public Enemies, and so designated them in my letter, sent to the Chief of Police, the Sheriff [and] every law enforcing officer. The purpose is to keep the publicity light shining on Chicago's most prominent, well known and notorious gangsters to the end that they may be under constant observation by the law enforcing authorities and law-abiding citizens."

It was not meant to be a list of people who were actively wanted by authorities for known crimes, just a list of people who were known criminals, and who should be watched. When J. Edgar Hoover became director of the Bureau of Investigation he appropriated the phrase, and used it to designate the fugitives he most wanted to have in custody, or dead. In 1950, list would become the Ten Most Wanted Fugitives List.

After the disastrous shootout at Little Bohemia, with his career hanging in the balance, Hoover decided to prioritize the Bureau's Public Enemies. The story goes that

Dillinger was given the designation of the Bureau's first Public Enemy Number One on his 31st birthday. "Pretty Boy" Floyd would replace Dillinger after his death, who would then be replaced by Dillinger's crime colleague Baby Face Nelson.

The heat was on like never before. The entire country was looking for Dillinger, Hamilton had just died, and Nelson had yet to return from his escape after Little Bohemia. This left Dillinger, Van Meter, and Carroll to have to scrounge up some money to evade the law by themselves. So they did what they did best.

Van Meter knew of a town in Ohio that was so unlike their usual hits they probably wouldn't even be suspected of the crime.

Fostoria was a railroad town that had as many as 140 trains slowly making their way through the center of town on a daily basis. Meticulous bank robbers like Herman Lamm would never plan a heist in a town that was practically inescapable.

Van Meter, though, had spent summers in the town as a child as was sure he knew the routes around town that would avoid the train tracks. He, Dillinger, and Carroll ditched their previous vehicle; blood-stained from Hamilton's shooting, in Chicago, hoping it would further throw off authorities.

They stole another car and made their way to Fostoria, Ohio. It was one of their most dangerous robberies yet. The men had learned to work in a five or six man team, but now they only had three, they also didn't do a test run, or know the layout of the bank, and the town was covered in train tracks where a train could block their escape route at every turn. But the men needed money and, as Van Meter said, if they pulled it off they probably wouldn't even be suspected.

Carroll was the getaway driver for this robbery, leaving Dillinger and Van Meter to go in alone. They were used to having lookouts at the door, and at least one other man in the building for crowd control. Not having cased the bank beforehand, the men didn't know there were two more exits inside the bank, one going to a jeweler store, and one to a drugstore.

A hostage, Frances Hillyard, managed to use one of the exits to escape the robbery, and she ran to find Frank Culp, the Chief of Police. Culp entered the lobby of the bank, hoping to use the mezzanine to fire down on the robbers. Van Meter noticed his entry, though, and immediately shot Culp in the chest with his machine gun.

Carroll heard shots from down the street where he waited in the getaway car. He got out and began firing wildly in the direction of the bank. Two civilians, Robert Shields, and R.W Powley, are hit by his barrage. Townspeople, who once delighted in watching a bank robbery happen, and thought of the outlaws as heroes, now gathered and shot at the men with their own guns.

Using their favorite escape tactic, Van Meter and Dillinger take two hostages, Bill Daub and Ruth Harris, and force them to accompany them outside, stand on the running boards of the car, and be their human shields until they get safely out of town.

The men made off with just over $17,000. Van Meter ended up being right when he said the authorities probably wouldn't even suspect the Dillinger Gang of the robbery, at least not initially.

Dillinger and Van Meter bought a red Ford truck with some of their heist money. They used it as a mobile safe house. Allegedly they outfitted it with mattresses in the back, and actually lived in it for several weeks, splitting their time between the truck and a dilapidated shack in the woods.

On the night of May 24th, 1934, Dillinger and Van Meter were driving the truck through a back road in East Chicago, Indiana, when a pair of policemen drove up. Van Meter decided there was no escaping the situation, and it was a choice between getting sent to jail, and shooting their way out.

He gunned Officers Martin O'Brien and Lloyd Mulvihill down with his Tommy gun before the men even had a chance to reach for their weapons, or exit the car. Their bodies were found later that day. Police just assumed it was the work of the Dillinger Gang because of the distinctive spray of machine gun bullets. The papers even reported that the man were "Slain in Dillinger Style"

One officer also noted that the dead men worked with Officer O'Malley and would be witnesses at Dillinger's murder trial if he were ever caught. This fact lent more credence to the idea that Dillinger shot the officers in cold blood. Dillinger later expressed remorse about this killing, saying they were just officers doing their jobs and they didn't deserve to die. Though, knowing it was him and Van Meter or the officers, it's unlikely he really regretted their deaths. He most likely saw them as unfortunate but necessary collateral damage.

Plastic Surgery

It was clear that the authorities were closing in on Dillinger. With these latest murders he was officially being blamed for crimes that police weren't even sure he committed. He needed to do something drastic. He asked his lawyers, Louis Piquett and Arthur O'Leary to find him a reliable plastic surgeon to alter his face enough that he would no longer be recognized.

On May 27th Dillinger moved into James Probasco's house. Probasco was a former boxer and member of a diamond heist ring. He was briefly trained as a veterinarian in his youth and now had a makeshift operating room in his home.

Piquett and O'Leary reached out to underworld doctor William Loeser, and his assistant Doctor Harold Cassidy. Both men had been in and out of trouble with the law for various reasons and needed the money they would get from the surgery.

Probasco had set the price of using his operating room and helping the lawyers finds the surgeons at $5,000 (over $90,000 in today's currency). Probasco had promised Loeser $1,700, while Cassidy was to get $1,200.

On May 28th the surgeons came to Probasco's house to begin surgery on Dillinger. John lied about how much he had eaten that day. This lead to the failure of the first attempt at anesthetizing Dillinger. In

Cassidy's second attempt he poured the entire bottle of ether onto the rag. Dillinger lost consciousness, but almost lost his life, too. He stopped breathing and began to turn blue before some primitive CPR tactics were used by Dr. Loeser which brought Dillinger back from the brink of death.

The surgery was brutal. Dillinger kept waking up from the anesthesia and vomiting, both from the ether overdose and the pure shock of being awake during a surgery. Over the course of several hours the doctors removed three moles from Dillinger's face, gave him a rudimentary face-lift, and filled in his famous cleft chin.

The doctors did what they could, but considering they were working in a makeshift operating room, not a hospital, and plastic surgery was actually relatively new at the time, they couldn't work miracles. However, Dillinger was initially pleased enough with the surgery to convince Van Meter to hand over his own $5,000 for the same procedure.

Later, once the swelling went down and he was mostly healed, Dillinger allegedly said, "Hell, I don't look any different than I did!"

The men soon realized they had another problem. Under the guidance of J. Edgar Hoover, America now had a centralized data bank of criminal fingerprints. It was the first era in history where your fingerprints could lead to your capture and arrest. This was bad news for Dillinger and Van Meter. Luckily for them, Dr. Loeser had recently invented a system of fingerprint removal.

He used a combination of nitric and hydrochloric acids in an excruciating procedure for which he charged the men an additional $100 per finger. After Dillinger's death, Loeser was found and made to testify about the work he did on Dillinger and Van Meter.

He described the fingerprint removal saying, "Cassidy and I worked on Dillinger and Van Meter simultaneously on June 3. While the work was being done, Dillinger and Van Meter changed off. The work that could be done while the patient was sitting up, that patient was in the sitting-room. The work that had to be done while the man was lying down, that patient was on the couch in the bedroom. They were changed back and forth according to the work to be done. The hands were sterilized, made aseptic with antiseptics, thoroughly washed with soap and water and used sterile gauze afterwards to keep them clean. Next, cutting instrument, knife was used to expose the lower skin...in other words, take off the epidermis and expose the derma, then alternately the acid and the alkaloid was applied as was necessary to produce the desired results."

Dillinger's autopsy showed that the procedure didn't completely work, and his fingerprints, while not completely intact, were still partially visible.

The Last Days of the Dillinger Gang

A few days after Dillinger and Van Meter's fingerprint surgeries, Tommy Carroll went to Waterloo, Iowa with his girlfriend, Jean Delaney. On June 7th, the couple stopped to gas up their car, then went to lunch. The gas station attendant had noticed several out-of-state license plates in the back seat, and reported the suspicious fact to the local police, along with the make and model of the car, and its current license number.

Detectives Emil Steffen and P.E. Walker drove around looking for the vehicle but had no luck until they returned to the station. Carroll had mistakenly parked across the street from the local police station. Carroll put up a fight when the detectives tried to arrest him and ended up getting shot four times. He later died of his wounds in St. Francis Hospital. Delaney, having been one of the women taken into custody after the Little Bohemia shootout, was arrested for violating her parole and given a year in jail.

All but three members of the Second Dillinger Gang were now dead and Dillinger feared the rest of them would be following closely behind their colleagues. With their funds depleted by the surgeries, and their eyes on a comfortable retirement in a tropical location, the gang planned one more big robbery.

Van Meter chose the Merchants National Bank in South Bend, Indiana. Done at the right time he figured the men could make off with $100,000. As many as three other men were brought on for the heist. Their identities have never been conclusively proven, though some speculate one could have been "Pretty Boy" Floyd, the man who took Dillinger's place as Public Enemy Number One after his death.

On June 30th, 1934 the men descended on South Bend. Van Meter was on lookout that day, while the others made their way into the bank. One of the unidentified men immediately began shooting up at the ceiling. The noise from the bank prompted Officer Howard Wagner to investigate. Van Meter saw him coming and shot him before he had the chance to get to the bank. He died on the scene.

The shooting set off a panic in the street. It was chaos as people ran for safety. Van Meter could hear sirens in the distance. Harry Berg, a local shop owner, grabbed his pistol from his shop and shot at one of the robbers.

Berg managed to hit Nelson who was not wounded due to his bulletproof vest, but was characteristically impulsive. He swung around and began firing wildly in the direction of the shooter. Many bullets shattered shop windows and car windshields. Bystanders were grazed with bullets and showered in shards of glass.

Joseph Pawlowski, a teenager who was passing by the scene, jumped on Nelson's back to try and stop him from shooting. Nelson struggled free, slamming Pawlowski into a glass window. The boy was shot in the hand by a stray bullet and passed out.

Police arrived on the scene and bullets continued to fly from both sides. The shootout racked up thousands of dollars in property damage, and wounded six civilians. Van Meter was grazed in the head by a police bullet. Dillinger and the gang got away as they usually did, by taking hostages from the bank. Among the hostages this time was the bank president.

The heist was not as fruitful as Van Meter had hoped. Not only did he get shot in the head, and murder a man, the gang only managed to steal $29,890, over $70,000 less than he was expecting.

The South Bend robbery ended up being the last recorded robbery for everyone known to have been, and suspected to have been involved. Less than a month later, Dillinger would be dead.

Betrayal and Death

After Billie's incarceration, John started dating 26-year-old Polly Hamilton, a waitress, and former prostitute at the brothel of Anna Sage. Hamilton and Sage stayed close, and were even living together at the time, along with Sage's son.

Anna Sage was actually Ana Cumpănaş, a Romanian madam, who ran a brothel in Gary, Indiana. She was being threatened with deportation for "low moral character". Desperate to find a way to stay in the country, Sage decided she would give the authorities what information she had on Dillinger.

Whether Sage knew her information would lead to Dillinger's death is unclear. It is certain, though, that she is the one who gave up Dillinger's location to authorities on the night he was killed.

She told Bureau agents that she, Polly, and Dillinger would be going to see a film on July 22nd, 1934. She was unsure whether the trio would go to the Biograph or Marbro theatre, but promised to get the information to the agents before the film. She also told them she would be wearing an orange dress, so they could more easily identify her, and thus, Dillinger.

When the day came, Sage, Hamilton, and Dillinger were spending time at Sage's house. She asked Dillinger where he wanted to go to the movie later, and he told her he wanted to go to the theater around the corner, meaning the Biograph.

Sage didn't have a phone, and wouldn't be able to make such a delicate phone call within earshot of Dillinger anyway. She told the couple she needed to quickly run to the store to get some butter for the fried chicken she was making for dinner. At the store, she called Melvin Purvis to inform him of the evening's plan.

Purvis and Hoover began mobilizing their men. Even with the tip from Sage they still thought it best to send agents to both theaters. They couldn't be totally sure that Sage was telling the truth, or that Dillinger wouldn't change his mind about what theater he wanted to go to. They wanted to leave no room for mistakes. Purvis and Hoover were fully determined to not let Dillinger slip through their fingers again.

At 8:30pm Dillinger, Hamilton, and Sage entered the Biograph Theater to see Clark Gable in the crime film Manhattan Melodrama. The studio later used the fact that Dillinger was taken out after he saw their film in order to promote it; a real-life crime drama coming to an end just steps away from their fictitious one.

Once they were sure Dillinger was in the Biograph, Purvis pulled the team from the Marbro Theater for extra manpower at the Biograph. Nobody wanted to risk letting Dillinger escape.

The Chicago police were not informed of the Bureau's plan to take down Dillinger. Purvis and Hoover not only wanted the glory for themselves, they also considered the Chicago PD to be inept, or possibly under Dillinger's thumb.

Some Chicago officers still showed up to the scene, though. They were called by a theater employee who, seeing so many men surrounding the theater, thought they were planning a robbery. Bureau agents had to quickly explain they were waiting on an important target, and that an obvious police presence might compromise the whole operation.

After the film Purvis waited in the doorway of the theater. Seeing Sage's orange dress as she, Polly, and Dillinger walked by, Purvis signaled the other agents by lighting a cigar. Many accounts say Dillinger looked Purvis right in the eye as he passed. He must have recognized the man who had been hunting him down for months because he then began to break away from Sage and Hamilton, and reach into his pocket for his pistol.

Dillinger made a break away from his dates and into a nearby alleyway. The Bureau had already blocked off this means of escape, but Dillinger was not about to just surrender to the authorities. Acting on orders to open fire on their target if he resisted arrest, three agents began shooting at Dillinger.

Herman Hollis, Clarence Hurt, and Charles Winstead all fired shots at Dillinger. In all the three men fired six bullets; Dillinger was shot four times and grazed twice. The bullet that killed him entered through the base of his neck, went through his spinal cord and brain, and exited just below his right eye. Dillinger fell on face first onto the ground.

An ambulance arrived shortly after the shooting, although it was clear Dillinger was already dead. He was officially pronounced dead at Alexian Brothers Hospital at 10:40pm, on July 22nd, 1934.

As a testament to his popularity, civilians on the scene supposedly dipped their handkerchiefs and skirt hems into Dillinger's blood as a souvenir. An estimated 15,000 people went to the Cook County morgue to visit his body, which was on display there for only a day and a half.

Rumors started to swirl that the man killed that night was not, in fact, John Dillinger. How could America's most notorious outlaw, a man who had escaped from jail twice, and evaded federal agents countless times, be brought down in such simple circumstances? People pointed to the difference in various facial features between pictures of Dillinger when he was alive, and what he looked like in death.

Of course, at the time, people may not have known that John underwent a crude plastic surgery in the hopes that he might be misidentified.

Only July 24th, Dillinger's body was sent back to his family in Indiana. Allegedly the hearse occasionally stopped along the way to display Dillinger's body to curious crowds. On July 25th, Dillinger's sister, Audrey, officially identified the body. John was given a funeral service, and was then buried in the family plot in Crown Hill Cemetery in Indianapolis, Indiana. There are still those who believe John Dillinger was not killed that night.

Dillinger's grave marker has had to be replaced three times since he was laid to rest, due to outlaw fans chipping pieces off of it to keep as a reminder of the legend buried beneath.

Conclusion

With Dillinger dead, the Outlaw Era was quickly coming to an end. Famous bank robbing duo Bonnie and Clyde were shot to death just two months before Dillinger.

Neither Baby Face Nelson, nor Homer Van Meter would survive until the end of the year, either. Van Meter was cornered by St. Paul authorities Chief Frank Cullen, Detective Tom Brown, and two other officers on August 23rd, 1934. He ran into an alleyway and fired two shots at the approaching men with his .45 caliber pistol. He was then riddled with bullets from police rifles and even submachine guns, prompting Van Meter's family to claim he was used as "target practice". He was buried in Fort

Wayne, Indiana, though the family did not give him a space in their family plot because of the shame he had brought to the Van Meter name.

Baby Face Nelson died the way he lived, in a violent and bloody gun battle. On November 27th, 1934, Nelson, his wife Helen, and an accomplice, John Paul Chase were driving on a highway near Chicago, when a Bureau vehicle housing agents Thomas McDade and William Ryan passed by, travelling in the opposite direction. Nelson and the agents recognized each other and began a bizarre pursuit that ended in Nelson tailing the agents instead of attempting to get away.

Another Bureau vehicle spotted Nelson and began pursuing him. In this vehicle was

Agent Samuel P. Cowley, and Agent Herman Hollis, one of the three men who fired at Dillinger on the day he died. Nelson had Helen drive to Barrington Park. The Bureau vehicle followed, and The Battle of Barrington began. By the end of the ensuing gun battle, Nelson and Hollis would be dead. Cowley died a few hours later from his wounds.

Like Tommy Carroll's girlfriend Jean Delaney, Helen Gillis had been arrested and released on parole after the Little Bohemia shootout. She was given a year in prison for harboring her husband.

From then on there was a shift in the minds of the American people. With most of the once-revered outlaws dead or in jail, and the threat of fascism looming over the world, people began to look at good and evil differently. Where they once saw outlaws as heroes who were standing up to the rich institutions that were stealing money from poor citizens, Americans now looked on outlaws as murderous criminals; relics of a bygone era.

The Federal Bureau of Investigation as we know it today was officially created out of the Bureau of Investigation and the Division of Investigation in 1935, partly due to the agents' stellar work catching and killing their Public Enemies.

The legend of John Dillinger has lived on in media portrayals since almost immediately following his death. The 1935 MGM film

Public Hero No. 1 included many details from Dillinger's life, including the shootout at Little Bohemia, a crude plastic surgery, and a shooting death in an alleyway outside a theater.

Many other films have been made about Dillinger's life since, including the most recent Public Enemies from 2009, starring Johnny Depp as John Dillinger.

The stories of these men and their other outlaw counterparts continue to fascinate people to this day. Perhaps people still see them as Robin Hood-type anti-heroes undermining the corrupt establishment. Maybe people long for a time when crime was almost elegant; committed by men and women with professionalism and style.

Regardless, the legendary John Dillinger will not soon be forgotten.

Printed in Great
Britain
by Amazon